PRINCIPLES OF DIALECTICS

PRINCIPLES OF DIALECTICS

ST. AUGUSTINE OF HIPPO

DALCASSIAN
PRESS
Dark Age & Medieval Texts

Translator: Curtin, D.P. (1985-)

ISBN: 979-8-3483-2898-6 (Paperback)
ISBN: 979-8-3483-2899-3 (eBook)
Library of Congress Control Number:

Printed by Ingram Content Group, 1 Ingram Blvd, La Vergne, Tennessee
First Printing 2024, Dalcassian Press, Wilmington, DE

This work is part of a series produced in association with the Scriptorium Project and its community of scholars and translators.
Please visit our website at: www.thescriptoriumproject.com

1

PRINCIPLES OF
DIALECTICS

CHAPTER I.-- On Simple Words.
Dialectics is the science of good disputation. We dispute, however, with words. Therefore, words are either simple or compound. Simple words signify one thing: for example, when we say man, horse, disputes, runs. Nor should you be surprised that "disputes," although composed of two parts, is still counted among the simple words. For a thing is illuminated by its definition. It has been said that that which signifies one thing is simple. Thus, we include in this definition that we do not include when we say, "I speak." For although it is one word, it does not have a simple meaning, since it also signifies the person who speaks. Therefore, it is already subject to truth or falsehood; for it can be denied or affirmed. Thus, every first and second person of the verb, although stated individually, will still be counted among compound words, which do not have a simple meaning. For whoever says, "I walk," signifies both the act of walking and himself who walks. And whoever says, "You walk," similarly signifies both the action being done and the one who is doing it. But indeed, whoever says, "He walks," signifies nothing other than the act of walking itself. Therefore, the third person of the verb will always be

counted among the simple words; and it cannot yet be affirmed or denied unless such words are used, to which the significance of the person is necessarily connected by the custom of speaking, as when we
say, "It rains" or "It snows," even if we do not add who rains or snows,
yet because it is understood, it cannot be counted among the simple
words.

CHAPTER II.-- Compound Words.

Compound words are those that signify several connected things,
as when we say, "The man walks," or "The man hurrying walks up
the mountain," and so on. But among compound words, some are
those that convey a complete thought, as those that have been said;
others do not convey a complete thought but expect something; as
the very same words we have said, if you subtract the word that is
placed, "walks," although the words are compound, "the man hurrying up the mountain," the statement still hangs. Therefore, separating
these words that do not complete the thought, we have those compound words that convey a complete thought: there are also two types
of these. Either the thought is conveyed in such a way that it is subject
to being held true or false, as in "Every man walks" or "No man walks,"
and similar statements. Or the thought is conveyed in such a way that,
although it fulfills the intention of the mind, it cannot be affirmed or
denied: as when we command, wish, or curse, and similar expressions.
For if someone says, "Go to the villa," or "I wish he would go to the
villa," or "May the gods destroy him," it cannot be argued that he is
lying, nor can it be believed that he is speaking the truth. For he has
neither affirmed nor denied anything; therefore, such statements do
not come into question or require a disputant.

CHAPTER III.-- Which are Simple Sentences, Which are Compound.

But those that are required are either simple or compound. Simple
sentences are those that are stated without any connection to another

sentence: as in the statement, "Every man walks." Compound sentences are those of which the connection is judged: as in "If he walks, he moves." But when a judgment is made about the conjunction of sentences, it lasts until it reaches a conclusion. The conclusion is that which is derived from the granted premises. What I mean is this: Whoever says, "If he walks, he moves," wants to prove something, so that with this granted, it remains true to say that he walks: and the conclusion follows, which cannot be denied, namely that he moves: which also cannot be granted, that is, that he does not walk. Again, if he wants to say in this way, "This man walks," it is a simple sentence: which if I grant, and add another that expects something for the completion of the sentence: "Whoever walks, moves." And even if I grant this, from this conjunction of sentences, although stated individually and granted, that conclusion follows, which must necessarily be granted, namely, therefore, this man moves.

CHAPTER IV.-- It Divides Compound Sentences.

Having briefly established these points, let us consider the individual parts. For there are the first two, one concerning those that are stated simply, where there is almost the matter of dialectics; the other concerning those that are stated compound, where the work appears. Those concerning the simple are called concerning speaking. However, that which concerns the compound is divided into three parts. For the separate conjunction of words that does not complete the thought, that which does complete the thought in such a way that it does not yet make a question or require a disputant, is called concerning eloquence. That which completes the meaning in such a way that judgments are made about simple sentences is called concerning prolocution. That which comprehends the thought in such a way that a judgment is made even about the very conjunction, until it reaches the conclusion, is called concerning the summation of prolocutions. Therefore, let us explain these individual parts more carefully.

CHAPTER V.-- How Matters, Words, Sayables, and Expressions are Treated in Logic. Sayable and expression differ.

The word is the sign of each thing, which can be understood by the listener, pronounced by the speaker. A thing is whatever is understood or felt or hidden. [For corporeal things are known, spiritual things are understood; however, God himself is hidden, and formless matter. God is that which is neither body, nor animal, nor sense, nor intellect, nor anything that can be conceived. Formless matter is the mutability of mutable things, capable of all forms.] A sign is also that which shows itself to the senses and something else to the mind. To speak is to give a sign with an articulated voice. I say articulated because it can be comprehended by letters. However, all these things that are defined, whether they are rightly defined, and whether until now the words of the definition have been pursued by other definitions, the place will indicate where the discipline of defining is treated. Now, what is at hand, take in attentively. Every word sounds. For when it is in writing, it is not a word, but a sign of a word. Indeed, when the letters are inspected by the reader, it occurs to the mind that it bursts forth in voice. For what else are written letters, but they show themselves to the eyes and voices to the mind? Because we have said a little earlier that a sign is that which shows itself to the senses and something else to the mind: what we read, therefore, are not words but signs of words. But as the letter itself, being the smallest part of an articulated voice, we abuse this term to call it a letter, even when we see it written; although it is completely silent, and no part of a voice is present, but a sign of a part of a voice appears: so too is a word called when it is written, although the sign of the significant voice does not shine forth. Therefore, as I began to say, every word sounds. But what sounds has nothing to do with dialectic. For it concerns the sound of a word when it is inquired or observed how much it is softened by the arrangement of vowels or bursts forth by collision; likewise, how consonants are knotted by interposition or roughened by accumulation; and how many or what syllables it consists of, where poetic rhythm and accents are treated solely by the business of ears. And yet when these are debated, there is no dialectic beyond this: for this knowledge is of disputing. But then words are signs of things when they have power over them; however, the words, those concerning which this is debated. For since we cannot speak of words except by words, and when we speak, we speak only of some things, it occurs to the mind that words are signs of things, so that things do not cease to be. Therefore, when a word proceeds from the mouth, if it proceeds for itself, that is, for something to be inquired about or debated about the word itself, it is indeed a thing subject to discussion and question. But the thing itself is called a word. Whatever is sensed not by the ear, but by the mind, and is held enclosed in the very mind, is called dicible: when, however, a word proceeds, not for itself, but for some other thing to be signified, it is called diction. The thing itself, which is no longer a word, nor the conception of a word in the mind, whether it has a word by which it can already be signified or does not have one, is called nothing other than a thing by its own proper name. Therefore, let these four be distinctly held: word, dicible, diction, thing. What I have said is a word, and the word is, and the word signifies. What I have said is dicible, it is a word; yet it is not a word, but signifies what is understood in the word and contained in the mind. What I have said is diction, it is a word, but such that now these two together, that is, the word itself, and what is made in the mind through the word, are signified. What I have said is a thing, it is a word, which signifies whatever remains beyond those three that have been said. But I see that this needs to be illustrated by examples. Therefore, let a certain grammarian ask a boy in this way: Arms, what part of speech is it? What has been said, Arms, has been said for itself, that is, a word for the word itself: however, the rest of what he says, what part of speech is it, is not for itself, but for the word that has been said, or is sensed in the mind, or is pronounced by voice. But when they are sensed in the mind, they are dicible before the voice; but when they burst forth into voice because of what I have said, they have become diction. The very arms, which here is a word, when pronounced by Virgil, was diction: for it was not pronounced for itself, but so that the wars which Aeneas waged, or the shield, or the other arms which Vulcan made for Aeneas might be signified. The very wars or arms, which were waged or brought by Aeneas; I say, those which when they were waged and existed were seen, and which if they were now present, we could either point to with a finger or touch, which even if they were not thought of, it does not mean that they were not: therefore, they are neither words, nor dicibles, nor diction by themselves; but they are things, which are now called things by their own proper name. Therefore, we must treat in this part of dialectic about words, about diction, about dicibles, about things: in all of which, since partly words are signified, partly not words (for there is nothing about which it is not necessary to dispute by words); thus it is first disputed about these, through which it is permitted to dispute about the others. Therefore, every word, except for sound, about which it is well disputed, pertains to the faculty of dialectic, not to the discipline of dialectic. Just as the defenses of Cicero are indeed of the rhetorical faculty, but not by these is the rhetoric itself taught.

CHAPTER VI.-- On the origin of the word. Where the word is said. The Stoics' opinion on the origin of the word.

Therefore, every word, because of what it sounds like, raises four necessary questions: its origin, its force, its declension, and its arrangement. The origin of the word is questioned when one asks why it is said in such a way: in my opinion, this is too curious and not very necessary. Nor did I find it pleasing to say this, as Cicero seems to think the same; for who needs authority in such a clear matter? But if it were indeed very helpful to explain the origin of a word, it would be foolish to undertake something that is surely infinite. For who can discover what was said and from where it was said? To this is added that, just as the interpretation of dreams is predicated upon each person's genius, so too is the origin of words. Indeed, someone thinks that words themselves are said because they seem to strike the ear: "Nay," says another, "because they strike the air." But our dispute is not great. For both derive the origin of this word from striking. But from the side, a third person brings in a quarrel: "For what is true," he says, "we ought to speak, and it is odious, nature itself judging, to lie; the word is named from the true." Nor did a fourth genius fail. For there are those who think the word is said from the true, but the first syllable is sufficiently noted, and the second ought not to be neglected. For when we say the word, they say, its first syllable signifies the true, the second the sound. However, they want this to be a "bomb." Hence Ennius called the sound of feet "the bomb of feet": and the Greeks say βοάσαι to shout; and Virgil, "The woods resound" (Georg. 3, v. 223). Therefore, the word is said as if from the true sounding, that is, from the true resonating. If this is so, this name prescribes indeed that when we make a word, we should not lie: but I fear that those who say these things may themselves be lying. Therefore, it now pertains to you to judge whether we should think the word is said from striking, or from the true alone, or from the true sounding; or rather, whether we should not care where it is said from, since we understand what it signifies. However, briefly I want you to take note of this place concerning the origin of words, lest we seem to have omitted any part of the work undertaken. The Stoics, whom Cicero mocks in this matter, assert that there is no word whose certain reason cannot be explained. And because in this way it was easy to suggest, if you said this is infinite; with what words you would interpret the origin of another word; again, its origin must be sought by you until it is reached so that the matter with the sound of the word harmonizes in some similarity, as when we say the tinkling of the air, the whinnying of horses, the bleating of sheep, the clangor of trumpets, the clanking of chains. For you perceive that these words sound in such a way that the things signified by these words resonate. But because there are things that do not sound; in these, the similarity of touch prevails, as if they touch the sense gently or harshly, the gentleness or harshness of the letters touches the hearing, thus they have produced names. And the very gentle, when we say it, sounds gently. Who would not judge harshness to be harsh by the very name? It is gentle to the ears when we say pleasure: it is harsh when we say cross. Thus, the things themselves affect, just as words are felt. Honey, as sweet as the thing itself tastes, so sweetly touches the name to the hearing. Bitter is harsh in both: wool and brambles, as the words are heard, so they are touched. They believed these to be like the cradles of words, so that the sense of things would harmonize with the sense of sounds. Hence the liberty of naming has proceeded to the similarity of the things themselves: so that when, for the sake of a word, the cross is said to be named because the harshness of the word itself harmonizes with the harshness of the pain which the cross causes: the legs, however, are not named because of the harshness of pain, but because in length and hardness they are more similar to the wood of the cross than to the other limbs, thus they have been named. From here, it has come to abuse, so that it is used not so much for a thing similar, but as if for a neighboring one. For what similarity is there between the signification of small and minute, when something can be small that is not only not minute but even has grown? We say, however, because of a certain proximity, minute for small. But this abuse of the word is in the power of the speaker: for it has small, so that it should not be said minute. That pertains more to what we want to show, which is that when a pool is said in baths, in which there is nothing of fish and nothing similar to fish, it seems to be named from fish because of the water, where fish have life. Thus, the word is not translated by similarity, but is used from a certain proximity. But if anyone says that men become similar to fish by swimming, and thus the name of the pool has arisen; it is foolish to refute this, since neither thing is abhorrent from the other, and both are hidden. However, it happens well that with one example we can now clarify what distinguishes the origin of a word, which is seized from proximity, from that which is drawn from similarity. Hence there has been a progression to the contrary. For a grove is thought to be named because it does not shine at all; and war, because it is not a warlike thing; and the name of a treaty, because it is not a foul thing: which if it has been named from the foulness of a pig, as some wish, it returns therefore to that proximity, when that which is done is named from that by which it is done. For this very proximity is altogether broad and is divided through many parts. Either through efficiency, as this itself is named from the foulness of a pig, through which a treaty is made; or through effect, as a well, which is believed to be named from its effect, drinking; or through that which contains, as a city, which they want to be named from the world, which is usually surrounded by a plow in auspicious places: of which Virgil also makes mention, where Aeneas designates the city with a plow (Aeneid 5, v. 755): or through that which is contained, as if someone affirms that a barn is named from barley with the letter d changed; or through abuse, as when we say barley, and there wheat is stored; or from a part the whole, as with the name of the point, which is the upper part of a sword, they call the whole sword; or from the whole a part, as hair is called as if it were a hair of the head. What further should I pursue? Whatever else can be added, whether by similarity of things and sounds, or by similarity of the things themselves, or by proximity, or by the contrary, you will see the origin of the word contained, which we cannot indeed pursue beyond the similarity of sounds; but we cannot always do this. For there are countless words whose reason cannot be given: or there is none, as I think; or it is hidden, as the Stoics contend. Yet see a little how they think to reach those cradles of words, or rather to the root and indeed the seed, beyond which they forbid seeking the origin, nor can anyone find anything if they wish. No one doubts the syllables in which the letter V occupies the place of a consonant, as they are in these words: belly, cunning, veil, wine, vomit, wound, thick and as if producing a strong sound. This is also approved by the custom of speaking, when we subtract them from certain words, lest they burden the ear. For hence we say you loved more willingly than you loved, and it went away; not it has not gone away; and in this way countless others. Therefore, when we say force, the sound of the word, as has been said, harmonizes strongly with the thing that is signified. Now from that proximity through what they effect, that is, because they are violent, the bonds can be seen to be named, and the vine by which something is bound. Hence vines, which hang by the ties by which they are bound. From here also because of similarity, Terence called the bent old man "the vine." Hence the earth, which is winding and trampled by the feet of travelers, is called a way. But if the way is believed to be named from the trampled way by the force of the feet, the origin returns to that proximity. But let us make it from the similarity of the vine or the withe, that is, being named from bending: therefore someone asks me why it is called a way: I answer, from bending, because the bent one was called a winding way by the ancients: hence they call the winding ones those which are surrounded by a wheel. It seeks to inquire from where the bent one is called bent: and here I answer, from the similarity of the vine. It presses and demands from where this name of vine is: I say because it binds that which it has encompassed. It inquires about binding itself, from where it is named: we will say, from force. If you ask why it is so called, the reason is rendered, because it harmonizes with a strong and robust sound with the word of the thing that is signified. Beyond what it requires, it has no further. However, in how many ways the origin of words is varied by the corruption of sounds, it is foolish to pursue: for it is both long, and less than what has been said, it is necessary.

CHAPTER VII.-- On the Power of Words.

Now let us briefly consider the power of words, as far as the matter allows. The power of a word is known by how much it can affect: it only has power to the extent that it can move the listener. Furthermore, it moves the listener either according to itself, or according to what it signifies, or from both together. But when it moves according to itself, it pertains either to mere sense, or to art, or to both. The sense is moved either by nature or by habit. Nature is moved in the case where someone is offended if the name Artaxerxes the king is mentioned, or is soothed when hearing Euryalus. For who, even if he has heard nothing about these men whose names are these, does not judge that in one there is the greatest harshness, and in the other there is gentleness? The sense is moved by habit when it is offended upon hearing something: for here it matters not whether it is a pleasant or unpleasant sound; yet the depths of the ears can be moved, whether they receive sounds passing through as known guests or unknown ones. The auditor, however, is moved by art when, upon hearing a word spoken to him, he pays attention to what part of the discourse it is, or if he has received anything else in those disciplines which are taught about words. Indeed, from both, that is, both sense and art, judgment about the word occurs when that which the ears measure is noted by reason, and the name is thus placed; as it is said, "the best": as soon as the ear is struck by one long syllable and two short ones of this name, the mind immediately recognizes the foot of the dactyl from art. The sense, however, does not move according to itself, but according to what the word signifies, when, upon receiving the sign through the word, the mind contemplates nothing other than the very thing of which that sign is what it has received: as when, upon the name Augustine being mentioned, nothing other than myself is thought of by him, to whom I am known; or any man comes to mind, if perhaps this name has been heard, whether he who does not know me, or he who knows another who is called Augustine. When, however, the word simultaneously moves the listener both according to itself and according to what it signifies; then both the utterance itself and that which is uttered are noticed together. Whence it happens that the purity of the ears is not offended when hearing, "He had torn apart with his hand, belly, penis, good country"; but it would be offended if a sordid and vulgar name were used for an obscene part of the body? In this, however, the deformity of both the sense and the mind would be offended, unless that ugliness of the thing which is signified is covered by the decorum of the significant word, when it is the same thing of which both terms are used: just as a prostitute is not different, but nevertheless appears differently in the attire with which she is accustomed to stand before a judge, than in the way she would lie in a luxurious chamber. Therefore, since such great and manifold power of words appears, which we have briefly touched upon for the time; a dual consideration arises from the sense: partly for the sake of explaining the truth, partly for the sake of preserving decorum, of which the first pertains to the dialectician, the second chiefly to the orator. For although it is not fitting for a dispute to be inept, nor for eloquence to be deceitful; yet in that, often and indeed almost always, the delights of listening disregard the desire to learn, and in this, the unskilled multitude considers what is said elegantly, even to be truly said. Therefore, when it becomes clear what is proper to each, it is evident that the disputant, if he has any care for delighting, should be sprinkled with rhetorical color; and the orator, if he wishes to persuade the truth, should be strengthened with dialectical, as it were, nerves and bones, which nature itself could neither take away from the firmness of our bodies nor allow to be exposed to the offense of the eyes. Thus, now for the sake of judging the truth, which dialectics professes, let us see what impediments arise from this power of words, of which we have scattered certain seeds.

CHAPTER VIII.-- Obscure and Ambiguous. Differences between the Obscure and the Ambiguous. Three Types of the Obscure.

Obscurity hinders the listener from seeing the truth in words, either through obscurity or ambiguity. The difference between the obscure and the ambiguous is that in the ambiguous, multiple meanings present themselves, of which it is unknown which should be preferred; in the obscure, however, nothing, or little that can be focused on, appears. But where little is apparent, the obscure is similar to the ambiguous: for example, if someone entering a path is met at some fork, or junction, or even, so to speak, at a multijunction, but due to the density of the fog, nothing of the paths is illuminated: therefore, they are first held back by obscurity from proceeding. But when the fog begins to thin somewhat, something can be seen, which makes it uncertain whether it is a path or merely a more distinct color of the ground: this is obscure, similar to the ambiguous. As the sky brightens enough for the eyes, the direction of all paths becomes clear; but whether to proceed is uncertain not due to obscurity, but due to ambiguity. Furthermore, there are three types of obscurities: one is that which is clear to the senses but closed to the mind; as if someone sees a pomegranate painted, who has neither seen it at any time nor heard what it is like; it is not a matter of the eyes, but of the mind, that they do not know what the painting represents. The second type is where the matter is open to the mind, unless it is closed to the senses, like a man painted in darkness: for when it is revealed to the eyes, the mind will not doubt that it is a painted man. The third type is one that is hidden even from the senses, which, if it were to play, would not emerge any more to the mind: this type is the most obscure of all, as if an unskilled person were compelled to recognize that painted pomegranate even in darkness. Now turn your mind to the words, of which these are the established similarities. Imagine a grammarian, having called his students together, and with silence established, has quietly said, "Temetum": those who were near enough heard it clearly; those who were further away heard it poorly; but those who were farthest away were not touched by the voice at all. Some of these knew what temetum was, namely those who, for some reason, were more distant; the rest were completely in the dark: all were hindered by obscurity. And here you can already see all those types of obscurities. For those who doubted nothing by hearing were suffering from that first type, which is similar to the pomegranate for the ignorant, but painted in the light. Those who knew the word, but received the sound either poorly or not at all; they were struggling with the second type, which is similar to the image of a man, but not in view, but in a completely dark place. But those who were not only devoid of the voice but also of the meaning of the word; they belonged to the third type, which is altogether the worst, being enveloped in blindness. What has been said, that something is obscure similar to the ambiguous, can be perceived in those who indeed knew the word, but had received no sound at all, or not a completely certain one. Therefore, anyone who wishes to avoid all obscure ways of speaking will use a voice that is clear enough, not hindered by the mouth, and will employ the most familiar words. Now see in the same example of the grammarian how much further ambiguity hinders than the obscurity of the word. For suppose those present heard the teacher's voice sufficiently, and that he pronounced a word that was known to all; for example, suppose he said, "Magnus," and then fell silent: consider what uncertainties arise upon hearing that name. What if he is about to ask, "What part of speech is it?" What if he intends to inquire about meters, "What is the foot?" What if he is about to ask a historical question, for example, "How many wars did the great Pompey wage?" What if he is about to say, for the sake of praising poems, "Magnus and almost alone the poet Virgil?" What if he is about to rebuke the negligence of the students, and then breaks forth into these words, "Magnus, you are seized by torpor due to lack of diligence?" Do you see the removed fog of obscurity, that which was previously said as if emerging from a multijunction? For this one thing that has been said, "magnus," is both a name, and a chorium foot, and Pompey is, and Virgil is, and the torpor of negligence. And if there are any other or innumerable things not mentioned, which can nevertheless be understood through this utterance of the word.

CHAPTER IX.-- Two types of ambiguities.

Therefore, it has been rightly said by dialecticians that every word is ambiguous. Nor should it be troubling that Hortensius accuses Cicero in this way: They say they hear ambiguities keenly, explain them clearly; likewise, they say that every word is ambiguous, how then will they explain ambiguities with ambiguities? For this is like bringing extinguished light into darkness. Indeed, it is easily and cleverly said.

But this is what Antonius says regarding Scaevola in the same Cicero: Finally, so that you may seem to speak clearly to the wise, even to the foolish you should speak truly. For what else does Hortensius do in that place, except with the sharpness of wit and charm of speech, as if with a magical and sweet cup he pours darkness upon the ignorant? For what has been said, that every word is ambiguous, has been said about individual words. Ambiguities are clarified through discussion, and no one discusses individual words, of course. Therefore, no one will explain ambiguous words with ambiguous words. And yet, since every word is ambiguous, no one will explain an ambiguous word except with words, but also with conjunctions, which are no longer ambiguous. For example, if it were said, "Every soldier is biped," it would not follow that the entire cohort consists of biped soldiers. Thus, when I say every word is ambiguous, I do not refer to a sentence, nor to a discussion, although these are woven with words. Therefore, every ambiguous word will not be explained by an ambiguous discussion. Now let us see the types of ambiguities. The first two are: one in those things that are spoken; the other in those things that are only written, causes uncertainty. For if someone hears "Acies," and if someone reads it, they may have uncertainty unless it is clarified by a sentence, whether it refers to the line of soldiers, or of iron, or of eyes, whether spoken or written. But if someone finds it written, for example, "leporem," and it is not clear what sentence it is placed in, they will certainly doubt whether the penultimate syllable of this word should be long, from "lepos"; or short, from "lepus." This would not allow ambiguity if it received the accusative case of this noun from the speaker's voice. But if someone says that the speaker could have mispronounced; then the listener would be impeded not by ambiguity, but by obscurity. However, from that same kind of ambiguity, because a word mispronounced in Latin does not lead the thinker into different interpretations, but pushes towards what appears. Therefore, since these two kinds greatly differ from each other, the first kind is again divided into two: for whatever is said, and can be understood in many ways, can be understood either by the same many with one word and one interpretation; or it is held by only one word, but explained in different ways. Those which can be included by one definition are called univocal; however, those which must be defined diversely under one name are called equivocal. Therefore, let us first consider univocal terms, so that as this kind has now been revealed, it may be illuminated by examples. When we say "man," we refer to a boy, a youth, an old man, a fool, a wise person, a great one, a small one, a citizen, a foreigner, an urbanite, a rustic, one who has been, as well as one who is now, one who is sitting, one who is standing, one who is rich, one who is poor, one who is acting something, one who is ceasing, one who is rejoicing, one who is mourning, or neither. But in all these expressions, there is nothing that does not receive the name of man, as it is also enclosed by the definition of man: for the definition of man is "rational animal, mortal": therefore, no one can say "rational mortal animal" only refers to a youth, nor also to an old man and a boy, etc., or that it is wise only, not also foolish; indeed, both these and others, which have been enumerated, are contained as by the name of man, so also by the definition: for whether boy, or fool, or poor, or even one who is sleeping, if he is not a rational mortal animal; he is not a man. But a man must necessarily be contained within that definition. And concerning the others, indeed nothing is ambiguous: but concerning a small boy or fool, or one who is completely foolish, or concerning a sleeping person, or a drunkard, or a madman, it can be doubted how they can be rational animals, even if it can be defended, but it is long to rush to other matters. For what is being discussed is sufficient, that this definition of man is not correct, unless every man is contained in the same, and nothing besides man. Therefore, these are univocal, which are enclosed not only by one name but also by one definition of the same name: although they can also be distinguished among themselves by their proper names and definitions. For different names, boy, youth, rich and poor, free and slave, and if there are any other differences, will have their own proper definitions among themselves: but as they have one common name "man," so the definition "rational animal, mortal" is one common definition.

2

LATIN TEXT

CAPUT PRIMUM.-- De simplicibus verbis.

Dialectica est bene disputandi scientia. Disputamus autem verbis. Verba igitur aut simplicia sunt, aut conjuncta. Simplicia sunt, quae unum quiddam significant: ut cum dicimus homo, equus, disputat, currit. Nec mireris quod, disputat, quamvis ex duobus compositum sit, tamen inter simplicia numeratum est. Nam res definitione illustratur. Dictum est autem id esse simplex, quod unum quiddam significet. Itaque hoc includimus hac definitione, quod non includimus eum dicimus, loquor. Quamvis enim unum verbum sit, non habet tamen simplicem significationem, siquidem significat etiam personam quae loquitur. Ideo jam obnoxium est veritati aut falsitati; nam et negari et affirmari potest. Omnis itaque prima et secunda persona verbi quamvis singillatim enuntietur, tamen inter conjuncta verba numerabitur, quae simplicem non habent significationem. Siquidem quisquis dicat, ambulo; et ambulationem facit intelligi, et seipsum qui ambulat. Et quisquis dicit, ambulas; similiter et rem quae fit, et eum qui facit, significat. At vero qui dicit, ambulat; nihil aliud quam ipsam significat ambulationem. Quamobrem tertia persona verbi semper inter simplicia numerabitur; et nondum aut affirmari aut negari potest, nisi talia verba sint, quibus necessario cohaeret personae significatio consuetudine loquendi, ut cum dicimus, pluit aut

ningit, etiamsi non addatur quis pluat aut ningat, tamen quia intelligitur, non potest inter simplicia numerari.

CAPUT II.-- Verba conjuncta.

Conjuncta verba sunt, quae sibi connexa res plures significant, ut
cum dicimus, homo ambulat, aut homo festinans in montem ambulat,
et si quid tale. Sed conjunctorum verborum alia sunt, quae sententiam
comprehendunt, ut ea quae dicta sunt; alia quae non comprehendunt,
sed exspectant aliquid; ut eadem ipsa quae diximus, si subtrahas verbum quod positum est, ambulat, quamvis enim verba conjuncta sint,
homo festinans in montem; tamen adhuc pendet oratio. Separatis igitur his verbis quae non implent sententiam, restant ea verba conjuncta quae sententiam comprehendunt: horum item duae species
sunt. Aut enim sic sententia comprehenditur, ut vero aut falso tenea-
tur obnoxia, ut est, omnis homo ambulat; aut, omnis homo non ambulat; et si quid hujusmodi. Aut sic impletur sententia, ut licet perficiat
propositum animi, affirmari tamen negarive non possit: ut cum im-
peramus, cum optamus, cum exsecramur, et his similia. Nam si quis
dicat, perge ad villam, vel utinam pergat ad villam, aut, dii illum per-
dant; non potest argui quod mentiatur, aut credi quod verum dicat.
Nihil enim affirmavit vel negavit: ergo nec tales sententiae in quaestionem veniunt, aut disputatorem requirunt.

CAPUT III.-- Quae simplices sententiae, quae conjunctae.

Sed illae quae requiruntur, aut simplices sunt, aut conjunctae. Simplices sunt, quae sine ulla copulatione sententiae alterius enuntiantur:
ut est illud quod dicimus, omnis homo ambulat. Conjunctae sunt de
quarum copulatione judicatur: ut est, si ambulat, movetur. Sed cum
de conjunctione sententiarum judicium fit, tamdiu est donec perveniatur ad summam. Summa autem est quae conficitur ex concessis.
Quod dico tale est, Qui dicit, Si ambulat, movetur, probare vult aliquid, ut hoc concesso, verum esse restet illi dicere, quod ambulet: et
summa consequatur, quae jam negari non potest, id est quod move-

tur: quae item non potest concedi, id est quod non ambulet. Rursus si hoc modo velit dicere, homo iste ambulat, simplex sententia est: quam si concessero, et aliam quae aliquid exspectat ad completionem sententiae adjunxerit: quisquis autem ambulat, movetur. Et hanc etiam si concessero, ex hac junctione sententiarum quamvis singillatim enuntiatarum et concessarum, illa summa sequitur, quae jam necessario concedatur, id est, igitur homo iste movetur.

CAPUT IV.-- Conjunctas sententias subdividit.

His igitur breviter constitutis, singulas partes consideremus. Nam sunt primae duae, una de iis quae simpliciter dicuntur, ubi est quasi materia dialecticae; altera de iis quae conjuncta dicuntur, ubi jam quasi opus apparet. Quae de simplicibus, vocatur de loquendo. Illa vero quae de conjunctis est, in tres partes dividitur. Separata enim conjunctione verborum quae non implet sententiam, illa quae sic implet sententiam, ut nondum faciat quaestionem vel disputatorem requirat, vocatur de eloquendo. Illa vero quae sic implet sensum, ut de sententiis simplicibus judicetur, vocatur de proloquendo. Illa quae sic comprehendit sententiam, ut de ipsa etiam copulatione judicetur, donec perveniatur ad summam, vocatur de proloquiorum summa. Has ergo singulas partes diligentius explicemus.

CAPUT V.-- Quomodo de rebus, verbis, dicibilibus, dictionibus, tractetur in logica. Differunt dicibile, et dictio.

Verbum est uniuscujusque rei signum, quod ab audiente possit intelligi, a loquente prolatum. Res est quidquid intelligitur vel sentitur vel latet. [Sciuntur enim corporalia, intelliguntur spiritualia; latet vero ipse Deus, et informis materia. Deus est quod neque corpus est, neque animal est, neque sensus est, neque intellectus est, neque aliquid quod excogitari potest. Informis materia est mutabilitas mutabilium rerum, capax omnium formarum.] Signum est et quod seipsum sensui, et praeter se aliquid animo ostendit. Loqui est articulata voce signum dare. Articulata autem dico quod comprehendi litteris potest. Haec autem omnia quae definita sunt, utrum recte definita sint, et utrum hactenus verba definitionis aliis definitionibus prosequenda fuerint, ille indicabit locus in quo definiendi disciplina tractatur. Nunc quod instat, accipe intentus. Omne verbum sonat. Cum enim est in scripto, non verbum, sed verbi signum est. Quippe inspectis a legente litteris, occurrit animo, quod voce prorumpat. Quid enim aliud litterae scriptae, quam seipsas oculis, et praeter se animo voces ostendunt? Quia et paulo ante diximus, signum esse quod seipsum sensui, et praeter se animo aliquid ostendit: quae legimus igitur, non verba sunt, sed signa verborum. Sed ut ipsa littera, cum sit pars minima vocis articulatae, abutimur tamen hoc vocabulo ut appellemus litteram, etiam cum scriptam videmus; quamvis omnino tacita sit, neque ulla pars vocis, sed signum partis vocis appareat: ita etiam verbum appellatur cum scriptum est, quamvis verbi signum significantis vocis non eluceat. Ergo, ut coeperam dicere, omne verbum sonat. Sed quod sonat, nihil ad dialecticam. De sono enim verbi agitur, cum quaeritur, vel animadvertitur, quanta vocalium vel dispositione leniatur, vel concursione dehiscat; item consonantium vel interpositione nodetur, vel congestione asperetur; et quot vel qualibus syllabis constet, ubi poeticus rhythmus accentusque a grammaticis solo aurium tractatur negotio. Et tamen cum de his disputatur, praeter dialecticam non est: haec enim scientia disputandi est. Sed tunc verba sunt signa rerum, quando de ipsis obtinent vim; verborum autem, illa de quibus hic disputatur. Nam cum de verbis loqui nisi verbis nequeamus, et cum loquimur non nisi de aliquibus rebus loquamur, occurrit animo ita esse verba signa rerum, ut res esse non desinant. Cum ergo verbum ab ore procedit, si propter se procedit, id est ut de ipso verbo aliquid quaeratur aut disputetur, res est utique disputationi quaestionique subjecta. Sed ipsa res verbum vocatur. Quidquid autem ex verbo non auris, sed animus sentit, et ipso animo tenetur inclusum, dicibile vocatur: cum vero verbum procedit, non propter se, sed propter aliud aliquod significandum, dictio vocatur. Res autem ipsa, quae jam verbum non est, neque verbi in mente conceptio, sive habeat verbum, quo jam significari possit, sive non habeat, nihil aliud quam res vocatur proprio jam nomine. Haec ergo quatuor distincte teneantur, verbum, dicibile, dictio, res. Quod dixi verbum, et verbum est, et verbum significat. Quod dixi dicibile, verbum est; nec tamen verbum, sed quod in verbo intelligitur et in animo continetur, significat. Quod dixi dictionem, verbum est, sed tale quo jam illa duo simul, id est ipsum verbum, et quod fit in animo per verbum, significantur. Quod dixi rem, verbum est, quod praeter illa tria, quae dicta sunt, quidquid restat, significat. Sed exemplis haec illustranda esse perspicio. Fac igitur a quodam grammatico puerum interrogatum hoc modo: Arma, quae pars orationis est? Quod dictum est, Arma, propter se dictum est, id est verbum propter ipsum verbum: caetera vero quod ait, quae pars orationis est, non propter se, sed propter verbum, quod arma dictum est, vel animo sensa, vel voce prolata sunt. Sed cum animo sensa sunt, ante vocem dicibilia sunt; cum autem propter id quod dixi, proruperunt in vocem, dictiones factae sunt. Ipsum vero arma, quod hic verbum est, cum a Virgilio pronuntiatum est, dictio fuit: non enim propter se prolatum est, sed ut eo significarentur vel bella quae gessit Aeneas, vel scutum, vel caetera arma, quae Vulcanus Aeneae fabricatus est. Ipsa vero bella vel arma, quae gesta sunt aut ingesta ab Aenea; ipsa, inquam, quae cum gererentur atque essent, videbantur, quaeque si nunc adessent, vel digito monstrare possemus, aut tangere, quae etiamsi non cogitarentur, non eo tamen fit ut non fuerint: ipsa ergo per se nec verba sunt, nec dicibilia, nec dictiones; sed sunt res, quae jam proprio nomine res vocantur. Tractandum est igitur nobis in hac parte dialecticae de verbis, de dictionibus, de dicibilibus, de rebus: in quibus omnibus cum partim verba significentur, partim non verba (nihil est enim de quo non verbis disputare necesse sit); itaque de his primo disputatur, per quae de caeteris disputare conceditur. Igitur verbum quodlibet, excepto sono, de quo bene disputatur, ad facultatem dialecticae pertinet, non ad dialecticam disciplinam. Ut defensiones Ciceronis sunt quidem rhetoricae facultatis, sed non his docetur ipsa rhetorica.

CAPUT VI.-- De origine verbi. Verbum unde dictum. Stoicorum de origine verbi opinio.

Ergo omne verbum propter id quod sonat, quatuor quaedam necessaria vocat in quaestionem, originem suam, vim, declinationem, ordinationem. De origine verbi quaeritur, cum quaeritur unde ita dicatur: res mea sententia nimis curiosa, et non nimis necessaria. Neque hoc mihi placuit dicere, quod sic Ciceroni quoque idem videtur; quamvis quis egeat auctoritate in re tam perspicua? Quod si omnino multum juvaret explicare originem verbi, ineptum esset aggredi, quod persequi profecto infinitum est. Quis enim reperire possit, quod quid dictum fuerit, unde ita dictum sit? Huc accedit, quod ut somniorum interpretatio, ita verborum origo pro cujusque ingenio praedicatur. Ecce enim verba ipsa quispiam ex eo putat dicta, quod aurem quasi verberent: Imo, inquit alius, quod aerem. Sed nostra non magna lis est. Nam uterque a verberando hujus vocabuli originem trahit. Sed e transverso tertius, vide, quam rixam inferat. Quod enim verum, ait, nos loqui oporteat, odiosumque sit, natura ipsa judicante, mendacium; verbum a vero cognominatum est. Nec ingenium quartum defuit. Nam sunt qui verbum a vero quidam dictum putent, sed prima syllaba satis animadversa, secundam negligi non oportere. Verbum enim cum dicimus, inquiunt, prima ejus syllaba verum significat, secunda sonum. Hoc autem volunt esse bombum. Unde Ennius sonum pedum, bombum pedum dixit: et βοάσαι Graeci clamare; et Virgilius, « Reboant silvae » (Georg. lib. 3, v. 223). Ergo verbum dictum est quasi a vero boando, hoc est verum sonando. Quod si ita est, praescribit quidem hoc nomen, ne cum verbum faciamus, mentiamur: sed vereor ne ipsi qui dicunt ista, mentiantur. Ergo ad te jam pertinet judicare, utrum verbum a verberando, an a vero solo, an a vero boando dictum putemus: an potius unde sit dictum non curemus; cum, quod significet, intelligamus. Breviter tamen hunc locum notatum esse de origine verborum, volo paulisper accipias, ne ullam partem suscepti operis praetermisisse videamur. Stoici autumant, quos Cicero in hac re irridet, nullum esse verbum, cujus non certa ratio explicari possit. Et quia hoc modo, suggerere facile fuit, si diceres hoc infinitum esse; quibus verbis alterius verbi originem interpretaveris; eorum rursus a te originem quaerendam esse donec perveniatur eo ut res cum sono verbi aliqua similitudine concinat, ut, cum dicimus, aeris tinnitum, equorum hinnitum, ovium balatum, tubarum clangorem, stridorem catenarum. Perspicis enim haec verba ita sonare, ut res quae his verbis significantur. Sed quia sunt res, quae non sonant; in his similitudinem tactus valere, ut si leniter vel aspere sensum tangunt, lenitas vel asperitas litterarum ut tangit auditum, sic eis nomina pepererit. Et ipsum lene cum dicimus, leniter sonat. Quis item asperitatem non et ipso nomine asperam judicet? Lene est auribus, cum dicimus voluptas: asperum est, cum dicimus, crux. Ita res ipsae afficiunt, sicut verba sentiuntur. Mel, quam suaviter res ipsa gustum, tam suaviter nomen tangit auditum. Acre, in utroque asperum est: lana et vepres, ut audiuntur verba, sic illa tanguntur. Haec quasi cunabula verborum esse crediderunt, ut sensus rerum cum sonorum sensu concordarent. Hinc ad ipsarum inter se rerum similitudinem processisse licentiam nominandi: ut cum, verbi causa, crux propterea dicta sit, quod ipsius verbi asperitas cum doloris, quem crux efficit, asperitate concordat: crura tamen non propter asperitatem doloris, sed quod longitudine atque duritia inter membra caetera sint ligno crucis similiora, sic appellata sint. Inde ad abusionem ventum est, ut usurpetur non tam rei similis, sed quasi vicinae. Quid enim simile inter significationem parvi et minuti, cum possit parvum esse, quod non modo nihil minutum sit, sed etiam aliquid creverit? Dicimus tamen propter quamdam vicinitatem, minutum pro parvo. Sed haec abusio vocabuli in potestate loquentis est: habet enim parvum, ut minutum non dicatur. Illud magis pertinet ad id quod volumus ostendere, quod cum piscina dicitur in balneis, in qua piscium nihil sit, nihilque piscibus simile habeat, videtur tamen a piscibus dicta propter aquam, ubi piscibus vita est. Ita vocabulum non translatum similitudine, sed quadam vicinitate usurpatum est. Quod si quis dicat homines piscibus similes natando fieri, et inde piscinae nomen esse natum; stultum est hoc refutare, cum ab re neutrum abhorreat, et utrumque lateat. Illud tamen bene accidit, quod uno exemplo dilucidare jam possumus, quid distet origo verbi, quae de vicinitate arripitur, ab ea quae similitudine ducitur. Hinc facta est progressio usque ad contrarium. Nam lucus dictus putatur, quod minime luceat; et bellum, quod res bella non sit; et foederis nomen, quod res foeda non sit: quod si a foeditate porci dictum est, ut nonnnulli volunt, redit ergo ad illam vicinitatem, cum id quod fit, ab eo per quod fit nominatur. Nam et ista omnino vicinitas late patet, et per multas partes secatur. Aut per efficientiam, ut hoc ipsum a foeditate porci, per quem foedus efficitur; aut per effectum, ut puteus, quod ejus effectus potatio est, creditur dictus; aut per id quod continet, ut urbem, ab orbe appellatam volunt, quod auspicato loco circumduci aratro solet: cujus rei et Virgilius meminit, ubi Aeneas urbem designat aratro (Aeneid. lib. 5, v. 755): aut per id quod continetur, ut si quis horreum mutata d littera affirmet ab hordeo nominatum; aut per abusionem, ut cum hordeum dicimus, et ibi triticum conditur; vel a parte totum, ut mucronis nomine, quae summa pars est gladii, totum gladium vocant; vel a toto pars, ut capillus quasi capitis pilus. Quid ultra provehar? Quidquid aliud annumerari potest, aut similitudine rerum et sonorum, aut similitudine rerum ipsarum, aut vicinitate, aut contrario, contineri videbis originem verbi, quam prosequi non quidem ultra soni similitudinem possumus; sed hoc non semper utique possumus. Innumerabilia enim sunt verba, quorum ratio reddi non possit: aut non est, ut ego arbitror; aut latet, ut Stoici contendunt. Vide tamen paululum, quomodo perveniri putant ad illa verborum cunabula, vel ad stirpem potius atque adeo sementum, ultra quod quaeri originem vetant, nec si quis velit, potest quidquam invenire. Nemo ambigit syllabas, in quibus V littera locum obtinet consonantis, ut sunt in his verbis, venter, vafer, velum, vinum, vomis, vulnus, crassum et quasi validum sonum edere. Quod approbat etiam loquendi consuetudo, cum quibusdam verbis eas subtrahimus, ne onerent aurem. Nam inde est quod amasti libentius dicimus quam amavisti, et abiit; non abivit; et in hunc modum innumerabilia. Ergo cum dicimus, vim, sonus verbi, ut dictum est, quasi validus congruit rei, quae significatur. Jam ex illa vicinitate per id quod efficiunt, hoc est quia violenta sunt, dicta vincula possunt videri, et vimen quo aliquid vinciatur. Inde vites, quod adminiculis quibus vinciantur nexibus pendent. Hinc etiam propter similitudinem, incurvum senem vietum Terentius appellavit. Hinc terra, quae pedibus itinerantium flexuosa et trita est, via dicitur. Si autem via, quae vi pedum trita est, creditur dicta, redit origo ad illam vicinitatem. Sed faciamus a similitudine vitis vel viminis, hoc est a flexu esse dictam: quaerit ergo me quispiam, quare via dicta est: respondeo, a flexu, quia flexum velut incurvum vietum veteres dixerunt: unde vietos quod cantho ambiantur, rotarum ligna vocant. Persequitur quaerere, unde vietum flexum dicatur: et hic respondeo, a similitudine vitis. Instat atque exigit unde istud sit vitis nomen: dico quia vincit ea quae comprehenderit. Scrutatur ipsum vincire, unde dictum sit: dicemus, a vi. Vis quare sic appellatur, requiret: redditur ratio, quia robusto et valido sono verbum rei, quae significatur, congruit. Ultra quod requirat non habet. Quot modis autem origo verborum corruptione vocum varietur, ineptum est prosequi: nam et longum, et minus quam illa quae dicta sunt, necessarium est.

CAPUT VII.-- De vi verbi.

Nunc vim verborum, quantum res patitur, breviter consideremus. Vis verbi est, qua cognoscitur quantum valeat: valet autem tantum, quantum audientem movere potest. Porro movet audientem, aut secundum se, aut secundum id quod significat, aut ex utroque communiter. Sed cum secundum se movet, aut ad solum sensum pertinet, aut ad artem, aut ad utrumque. Sensus autem aut natura movetur, aut consuetudine. Natura movetur in eo, quod offenditur si quis nominet Artaxerxem regem, vel mulcetur cum audit Euryalum. Quis enim etiamsi nihil utique de his hominibus audierit, quorum ista sunt nomina, non tamen in illo asperitatem maximam, et in hoc judicet esse lenitatem? Consuetudine movetur sensus, cum offenditur cum audit quiddam: nam hic ad suavitatem soni vel insuavitatem nihil interest;

sed tamen valent aurium penetralia movere, utrum per se transeuntes
sonos quasi hospites notos, an ignotos recipiant. Arte autem movetur
auditor, cum enuntiato sibi verbo, attendit quae sit pars orationis, vel
si quid aliud in his disciplinis, quae de verbis traduntur, accepit. At
vero ex utroque, id est et sensu et arte de verbo judicatur, cum id,
quod aures metiuntur, ratio notat, et nomen ita ponitur; ut dicitur,
optimus: mox ut aurem longa una syllaba et duae breves hujus nominis
percusserint, animus ex arte statim pedem dactylum agnoscit. Sensum
vero non secundum se, sed secundum id quod significat verbum
movet, quando per verbum accepto signo, animus nihil aliud quam ipsam rem intuetur, cujus illud signum est quod accepit: ut cum, Au-
gustino nominato, nihil aliud quam ego ipse cogitor ab ipso, cui notus
sum: aut quilibet hominum menti occurrit, si forte hoc nomen, vel
qui me ignorat audierit, vel qui alium novit, qui Augustinus vocetur.
Cum autem simul et secundum se verbum movet audientem, et secundum id quod significat; tunc et ipsa enuntiato, et id quod ab eo enun-
tiatur, simul advertitur. Unde enim fit quod non offenditur aurium
castitas, cum audit, Manu, ventre, pene, bona patria laceraverat; of-
fenderetur autem si obscoena pars corporis sordido ac vulgari nomine
appellaretur? in hoc autem sensum animumque utriusque deformi-
tas offenderet, nisi illa turpitudo rei quae significata est, decore verbi
significantis operiretur, cum res eadem sit, cujus utrumque vocabulum est: veluti non alia meretrix, sed aliter tamen videtur eo cultu,
quo ante judicem stare assolet, aliter eo quo in luxuriosi cubiculo jac-
eret. Cum igitur tantam vim tamque multiplicem appareat esse verborum, quam breviter pro tempore summatimque attigimus; duplex hic
ex consideratione sensus nascitur: partim propter explicandam veritatem, partim propter servandum decorem, quorum primum ad di-
alecticum, secundum ad oratorem maxime pertinet. Quamvis enim
nec disputationem deceat ineptam, nec eloquentiam oporteat esse
mendacem; tamen et in illa saepe atque adeo pene semper audiendi
delicias discendi cupido contemnit, et in hac imperitior multitudo
quod ornate dicitur, etiam vere dici arbitratur. Ergo cum appareat

quid sit uniuscujusque proprium, manifestum est et disputatorem, si qua ei delectandi cura est, rhetorico colore aspergendum; et oratorem, si veritatem persuadere vult, dialecticis quasi nervis atque ossibus esse roborandum, quae ipsa natura corporibus nostris, nec firmitati virium subtrahere potuit, nec oculorum offensioni patere permisit. Itaque nunc propter veritatem dijudicandam, quod dialectica profitetur, ex hac verborum vi, cujus quaedam semina sparsimus, quae impedimenta nascantur videamus.

CAPUT VIII.-- Obscurum et ambiguum. Differentiae obscuri et ambigui. Tria genera obscurorum.

Impedit auditorem ad veritatem videndam in verbis, aut obscuritas aut ambiguitas. Inter obscurum et ambiguum hoc interest, quod in ambiguo plura se ostendunt, quorum quid potius accipiendum sit ignoratur; in obscuro autem nihil, aut parum quod attendatur, apparet. Sed ubi parum est quod apparet, obscurum est ambiguo simile: veluti si quis ingrediens iter, excipiatur aliquo bivio, vel trivio, vel etiam, ut ita dicam, multivio loco, sed densitate nebulae nihil viarum quod est, eluceat: ergo a pergendo prius obscuritate tenetur. At ubi aliquantum rarescere nebulae coeperint, videtur aliquid, quod utrum via sit, an terrae proprius et nitidior color incertum est: hoc est obscurum ambiguo simile. Dilucescente coelo quantum oculis satis sit, jam omnium viarum deductio clara est; sed qua sit pergendum, non obscuritate, sed ambiguitate dubitatur. Item sunt obscurorum genera tria: unum est quod sensui patet, animo clausum est; tanquam si quis malum punicum pictum videat, qui neque viderit aliquando, nec omnino quale esset audierit; non oculorum est, sed animi, quod cujusce rei pictura sit, nescit. Alterum genus est, ubi res animo pateret, nisi sensui clauderetur, sicut est homo pictus in tenebris: nam ubi oculis apparuerit, nihil animus hominem pictum dubitabit. Tertium genus est, in quo etiam sensui absconditur, quod tamen si ludaretur, nihilo magis animo emineret: quod genus est omnium obscurissimum, ut si imperitus malum illud punicum pictum etiam in tenebris cogeretur agnoscere. Refer nunc animum ad verba, quorum istae sunt similitudines constitutae. Pone quempiam grammaticum, convocatis discipulis, factoque silentio suppressa voce dixisse, Temetum: quod ab eo dictum, qui prope assidebant, satis audierunt; qui remotius, parum; qui autem remotissime nulla omnino voce perstricti sunt. Horum autem partim sciebant, illi scilicet qui nescio quo casu remotiores erant, quid esset temetum; reliquos prorsus latebat: omnes obscuritate impediebantur. Et hic jam perspicis omnia illa genera obscuritatum. Nam qui auditu nihil dubitabant, primum illud genus patiebantur, cui simile est, malum punicum ignorantibus, sed in luce pictum. Qui noverant verbum, sed auribus aut parum aut omnino non acceperant vocem; secundo illo genere laborabant, cui similis est hominis imago, sed non in conspicuo, sed omnino tenebroso loco. Qui autem non solum vocis, sed et significationis verbi expertes erant; tertii generis, quod omnino deterrimum est, caecitate involvebantur. Quod autem dictum est, quoddam obscurum ambiguo simile, in his perspici potest, quibus verbum erat quidem notum, sed vocem penitus nullam, aut non omnino certam perceperant. Omnia igitur obscura loquendi genera vitabit, qui et voce quantum satis est clara, nec ore impedito, et verbis notissimis utetur. Vide nunc in eodem grammatici exemplo, quam longe alias impediat ambiguitas quam obscuritas verbi. Fac enim eos qui aderant et satis sensu accepisse vocem magistri, et illum verbum enuntiasse, quod esset omnibus notum; ut puta, fac eum dixisse, Magnus, et deinde siluisse: attende quid incerti, hoc audito nomine, patiantur. Quid si dicturus est, Quae pars orationis est? Quid si de metris quaesiturus, qui sit pes? Quid si historiam interrogaturus, ut puta, magnus Pompeius quot bella gesserit? Quid si commendandorum carminum gratia dicturus est, Magnus et pene solus poeta Virgilius? Quid si objurgaturus negligentiam discipulorum, in haec deinde verba prorumpat, Magnus vos ob studium disciplinae torpor invasit? Videsne remota nebula obscuritatis, illud quod supra dictum est quasi eminuisse multivium? Nam hoc unum quod dictum est, magnus, et nomen est, et pes chorius est, et Pompeius est, et Virgilius est, et negligentiae torpor. Et si qua alia vel innumerabilia non commemorata sunt, quae tamen per hanc enuntiationem verbi possunt intelligi.

CAPUT IX.-- Ambiguitatum genera duo.

Itaque rectissime a dialecticis dictum est, ambiguum esse omne verbum. Nec moveat quod apud Ciceronem calumniatur Hortensius, hoc modo: Ambigua se aiunt audire acute, explicare dilucide: item omne verbum ambiguum esse dicunt, quomodo igitur ambigua ambiguis explicabunt? nam hoc est in tenebras exstinctum lumen inferre. Facile quidem atque callide dictum. Sed hoc est quod apud eumdem Ciceronem Scaevolae dicit Antonius: Denique ut sapientibus diserte, stultis etiam vere videaris dicere. Quid enim aliud loco illo facit Hortensius, nisi acumine ingenii et lepore sermonis, quasi meraco et suavi poculo imperitis caliginem offundit? Quod enim dictum est, omne verbum ambiguum esse, de singulis verbis dictum est. Explicantur ambigua disputando, et nemo utique verbis singulis disputat. Nemo igitur ambigua verba verbis ambiguis explicabit. Et tamen cum omne verbum ambiguum sit, nemo verbum ambiguum nisi verbis, sed etiam conjunctis, quae jam ambigua non sunt, explicabit. Ut enim si diceretur. Omnis miles bipes est, non ex eo sequeretur, ut cohors ex militibus bipedibus tota constaret. Ita cum dico ambiguum omne verbum, non dico sententiam, non disputationem quamvis verbis ista texantur. Omne igitur ambiguum verbum non ambigua disputatione explicabitur. Nunc ambiguitatum genera videamus. Quae prima duo sunt: unum in iis etiam, quae dicuntur; alterum quod in iis solis, quae scribuntur, dubitationem facit. Nam si quis audierit, Acies, et si quis legerit, poterit incertum habere, nisi per sententiam clarescat, utrum acies militum, an ferri, an oculorum dicta vel scripta sit. At vero si quis inveniat scriptum, verbi causa leporem, nec appareat qua sententia positum sit, profecto dubitabit, utrum penultima hujus verbi syllaba producenda sit, ab eo quod est lepos; an ab eo quod est lepus corripienda. Quam scilicet non pateretur ambagem, si accusativum hujus nominis casum voce loquentis acciperet. Quod si quis dicat, lo-

quentem male pronuntiare potuisse; jam non ambiguitate, sed obscuritate impediretur auditor. Ex illo tamen genere quod ambigno simile
est, quia male latine pronuntiatum verbum, non in diversas rationes
trahit cogitantem, sed ad id quod apparet impellit. Cum igitur ista
duo genera inter se plurimum distent, primum genus rursus in duo dividitur: nam quidquid dicitur, et per plura intelligi potest, eadem scilicet plura aut uno vocabulo et una interpretatione; aut tantum uno
tenentur vocabulo, sed diversis expeditionibus explicantur. Ea quae
una definitio potest includere, univoca nominantur: illis autem quae
sub uno nomine necesse est definire diverse, aequivoci nomen est.
Prius ergo consideremus univoca, ut quomodo genus hoc jam pate-
factum est, illustretur exemplis. Hominem cum dicimus, tam puerum
dicimus quam juvenem, quam senem, tam stultum quam sapientem,
tam magnum quam parvum, tam civem quam peregrinum, tam ur-
banum quam agrestem, tam qui jam fuit quam qui nunc est, tam
sedentem quam stantem, tam divitem quam pauperem, tam agentem
aliquid quam cessantem, tam gaudentem quam moerentem vel neutrum. Sed in his omnibus dictionibus nihil est, quod non ut hominis
nomen accepit, ita etiam hominis definitione claudatur: nam definitio hominis est, Animal rationale, mortale: non ergo quisquam potest
dicere animal rationale mortale juvenem tantum, non etiam senem et
puerum, etc., aut sapientem esse tantum, non etiam stultum; imo et
ista et caetera, quae numerata sunt, sicut hominis nomine, ita etiam
definitione continentur: nam sive puer, sive stultus, sive pauper, sive
etiam dormiens, si animal rationale mortale non est; nec homo est.
Est autem homo; illa igitur definitione contineatur necesse est. Et de
caeteris quidem nihil ambigitur: de puero autem parvo aut stulto, sive
prorsus fatuo, aut de dormiente, vel ebrio, vel furente dubitari potest,
quomodo possunt esse animalia rationalia, etiam si possit defendi, sed
ad alia properantibus longum est. Ad id quod agitur illud satis est,
non esse istam definitionem hominis rectam, nisi et omnis homo eadem contineatur, et praeter hominem nihil. Haec sunt igitur univoca,
quae non solum nomine uno, sed una etiam ejusdem nominis defi-

nitione clauduntur: quamvis et inter se propriis nominibus et definitionibus distingui possunt. Diversa enim nomina, puer, adolescens,
dives et pauper, liber et servus, et si quod aliud differentiarum est, et
inter se ideo proprias definitiones habebunt: sed ut illis unum com-
mune nomen est homo, sic animal rationale mortale definitio una
communis est.

CAPUT X.-- Ambiguitas ex aequivocis varia.

Nunc aequivoca videamus, in quibus ambiguitatum perplexio
prope infinita silvescit: conabor tamen eas in genera certa distinguere.
Utrum autem conatum meum haec facultas sequatur, tu judicabis.
Ambiguitatum igitur, quae ab aequivocis veniunt, primo genera tria
sunt: unum ab arte, alterum ab usu, tertium ab utroque. Arte nunc
dico, propter nomina quae in verborum disciplinis verbis imponun-
tur. Aliter enim definitur apud grammaticos quid sit aequivocum,
aliter apud dialecticos; et tamen hoc unum quod dico, Tullius, et
nomen est, et pes dactylus, et aequivocum. Itaque si quis ex me ef-
flagitet, ut definiam quid sit Tullius, cujuslibet notionis explicatione
respondeo. Possum enim recte dicere, Tullius nomen est, quo significatur homo summus quidam orator, qui Catilinae conjurationem con-
sul oppressit. Subtiliter attende me nomen ipsum definisse: nam si
mihi Tullius ipse, qui si viveret, digito monstrari potuisset, definien-
dus foret, non dicerem, Tullius est nomen, quo significatur homo; sed
dicerem, Tullius est homo, et ita caetera adjungerem. Item respondere
possum, Hoc nomen Tullius est dactylus, his litteris constans: quod
enim eas litteras habeat, opus est innuere. Licet enim illud dicere,
Tullius est verbum, per quod aequivocantur inter se omnia cum hoc
ipso, quae supra dicta sunt, et si quid aliud inveniri potest. Sed dico,
Cum ergo hoc nomen quod dixi, Tullius, secundum artium vocabula
tam varie mihi licuit definire; quid dubitamus esse ambiguorum genus
ex aequivocis venientium, quod merito dici possit ex arte contingere?
Diximus enim aequivoca esse, quae non ut uno nomine, ita etiam una
definitione possunt teneri. Unde nunc alterum genus est, quod ex lo-

quendi usu venire memoravimus. Usum nunc appello illud verbum, propter quod verba cognoscimus. Quis enim verba propter verba conquirat et colligat? Itaque jam constitue aliquem sic audire, ut notum ei sit, nihil de partibus orationis, aut de metris quaeri, aut de verborum aliqua disciplina: tamen adhuc potest cum dicitur, Tullius, aequivocorum ambiguitate impediri. Hoc enim nomine et ipse qui fuit summus orator, et ejus picta imago vel statua, et codex quo ejus litterae continentur, et si quid est in sepulcro ejus cadaveris, significari potest. Diversis enim rationibus dicimus, Tullius ab interitu patriam liberavit; et, Tullius inauratus in Capitolio stat; et, Tullius, tibi totus legendus est; et, Tullius hoc loco sepultus est: unum enim nomen est, sed diversis haec omnia definitionibus explicanda sunt. Hoc igitur genus aequivocorum est, in quo jam nulla de disciplina verborum oritur ambiguitas, sed de ipsis rebus quae significantur. At si utrumque confundat audientem vel legentem, sive quod ex arte, sive ex loquendi usu dicitur, nonne tertium genus recte annumerabitur? Cujus exemplum in sententia quidem apertius apparet, ut si quis dicat, Multi dactylico metro scripserunt, ut est Tullius: nam hic incertum est utrum Tullius pro exemplo dactyli pedis, an dactylico poetae positum sit: quorum illud ex arte, hoc ex usu loquendi accipitur. Sed in simplicibus etiam verbis contingit, licet tantum vocem hujus verbi grammaticus audientibus discipulis enuntiet, ut supra ostendimus. Cum igitur haec tria genera manifestis rationibus inter se differant, rursum primum genus in duo dividitur. Quidquid enim ex arte, verborum facit ambiguitatem, partim sibi pro exemplo esse potest, partim non potest. Cum enim definio quid significat nomen, possum hoc ipsum exempli gratia supponere, quod dico nomen, utique nomen est: hac enim lege per casus flectitur dicendo nomen, nominis, nomini, etc. Item cum definio quid significat, dactylus, hoc ipsum potest pro exemplo esse: etenim cum dicimus, dactylus, unam syllabam longam et duas deinde breves enuntiamus. At vero cum definitur adverbium quid significet, non potest hoc ipsum pro exemplo dici: etenim cum adverbium dicimus, haec ipsa enuntiatio nomen est. Ita secundum aliam notionem, adverbium utique adverbium est, et nomen non est; secundum aliam vero adverbium non est adverbium, quia nomen est. Item pes creticus, quando quid significet definitur, non potest hoc ipsum pro exemplo esse: haec enim ipsa enuntiatio quando dicimus, creticus, prima longa syllaba, deinde duabus brevibus constat; quod autem significat, longa syllaba et brevis et longa est: ita et hic secundum aliam notionem, creticus nihil aliud est quam creticus, et dactylus non est; secundum aliam vero creticus non est creticus, quia dactylus est. Secundum igitur genus, quod jam propter disciplinas verborum ad loquendi usum dictum est pertinere, duas habet formas. Nam aequivoca dicta sunt, aut ex eadem origine venientia, aut ex diversa. Ex eadem origine appello, quando uno nomine ac non sub una definitione teneantur, uno tamen quasi fonte dimanant, ut est istud, quia Tullius et homo et statua et codex et cadaver intelligi potest: non possunt quidem ista una definitione concludi, sed tamen unum habent fontem, ipsum scilicet verum hominem, cujus et illa statua, et ille liber, et illud cadaver est. Ex diversa origine, ut cum dicimus, nepos, longe ex diversa origine filium filii et luxuriosum significat. Haec ergo distincta teneamus, et inde illud genus, quod ex eadem origine appello, in quae item dividatur: nam dividitur in duo, quorum unum translatione, alterum declinatione contingit. Translationem voco, cum vel similitudine unum nomen fit multis rebus, ut Tullius, et ille in quo magna eloquentia fuit, et statua ejus dicitur. Vel ex toto, cum pars cognominatur, ut cum cadaver illius Tullius dici potest: vel ex parte totum, ut cum tecta dicimus totas domus. Aut a genere species: verba enim principaliter dicunt Romani, quibus loquimur; sed tamen verba proprie nominata sunt, quae per modos et tempora declinamus: aut ab specie genus; nam cum scholastici non solum proprie, sed et primitus dicantur ii qui adhuc in schola sunt; omnes tamen qui in litteris vivunt, nomen hoc usurpant. Aut ab efficiente effectus, ut Cicero est liber Ciceronis: aut ab effectu efficiens, ut terror, quia terrorem fecit. Aut a continente quae continentur, ut domus etiam qui in domo sunt dicuntur: aut a conversa vice, ut castanea arbor dicitur quae et fructus: vel si quod aliud inveniri potest, quod ex eadem origine quasi transferendo cognominetur. Vides, ut arbitror, quid faciat in verbis ambiguitatem. Quae autem ad eamdem originem pertinentia conditione declinationis ambigua esse dicimus, talia sunt. Fac verbi causa quemque dixisse, pluit. Et haec diverse utique definienda sunt. Item scribere cum dicit, incertum est utrum in infinitivo activi, an imperativo passivi pronuntiatum sit. Homo cum unum nomen sit, et una enuntiatio, tamen fit aliud ex nominativo, aliud ex vocativo. Quin doctius et docte verbi enuntiatio quoque diversa est. Doctius aliud est cum dicimus, doctius mancipium; aliud cum dicimus, doctius illo disputavit. Declinatione igitur ambiguitas orta est: nam declinationem nunc appello, quidquid sive per voces sive per significationes flectendo verba contingit. Hic doctus et docte, tantum per voces flexum est; hic homo et homo, secundum solas significationes. Sed hujusmodi genus ambiguitatum minutatim concidere ac prosequi pene infinitum est. Itaque locum ipsum hactenus notasse suffecerit, ingenio praesertim tuo. Vide nunc ea, quae ex diversa origine veniunt: nam ipsa dividuntur adhuc in duas primas formas, quarum una est, quae contingit diversitate linguarum; ut cum dicimus, iste, haec una vox aliud apud Graecos, aliud apud nos significat. Quod genus tamen non omnis novit: non enim unicuique perspicuum est, nisi qui linguas nosset, aut qui linguas disputaret. Altera forma est, quae in una quidem lingua facit ambiguitatem, diversa tamen eorum origine, quae uno vocabulo significantur, quale est illud, quod de nepote supra posuimus. Quod rursus in duo scinditur Aut sub eodem genere partis orationis, sicut nomen est nepos, cum filium filii, et cum luxuriosum significat; aut sub diversis, ut dictum est a Terentio, Qui scias ergo istuc nisi periclum feceris? (Terent. Andr. act. 3, scen. 3, v. 33.) sed etiam istuc pronomen, istuc adverbium. Jam ex utroque, id est arte et usu verborum, quod in aequivocis tertium genus posueramus, tot ambiguitatum formae possunt existere, quot in duobus superioribus posueramus. Restat ergo illud genus ambiguum: quod in scriptis solis reperitur. Cujus tres sunt species: aut enim spatio syllabarum fit tale ambiguum, aut acumine, aut utroque. Spatio autem, ut cum scribitur, venit, de tempore incertum est, propter occultum primae syllabae spatium. Acumine autem, ut cum scribitur, pone, utrum ab eo quod est pono, an ut dictum: Pone sequens, namque hanc dederat Proserpina legem. (Georg. liv. 4, v. 487.) incertum est propter latentem acuminis locum. A vero ex utroque fit, ut in superioribus de lepore diximus; nam non solum producenda, sed acuenda est etiam penultima syllaba hujus verbi, si ab eo quod est lepos, non ab eo quod est lepus, deflexum est.

This work was produced in
association with:

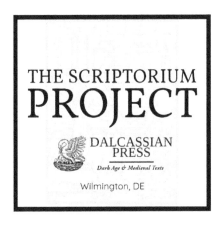